Crisis Actor

Crisis Actor

POEMS

Declan Ryan

FARRAR, STRAUS AND GIROUX

NEW YORK

Farrar, Straus and Giroux
120 Broadway, New York 10271

Copyright © 2023 by Declan Ryan
All rights reserved
Printed in the United States of America
Originally published in 2023 by Faber & Faber Ltd, Great Britain
Published in the United States by Farrar, Straus and Giroux
First American edition, 2024

Library of Congress Cataloging-in-Publication Data
Names: Ryan, Declan, 1983– author.
Title: Crisis actor : poems / Declan Ryan.
Description: First American edition. | New York : Farrar, Straus
  and Giroux, 2024.
Identifiers: LCCN 2023038969 | ISBN 9780374611897 (hardcover)
Subjects: LCGFT: Poetry.
Classification: LCC PR6118.Y3537 C75 2024 | DDC 821/.92—
  dc23/eng/20230928
LC record available at https://lccn.loc.gov/2023038969

Our books may be purchased in bulk for promotional,
educational, or business use. Please contact your local bookseller
or the Macmillan Corporate and Premium Sales Department at
1-800-221-7945, extension 5442, or by email at
MacmillanSpecialMarkets@macmillan.com.

www.fsgbooks.com
Follow us on social media at @fsgbooks

1   3   5   7   9   10   8   6   4   2

Some day they're gonna write a blues for fighters.
It'll just be for slow guitar, soft trumpet and a bell.

— SONNY LISTON

Contents

Crisis Actor

Sidney Road

A lookout on the world: next door's wisteria,
its purple leaching out, half hides
a railing that needs paint;
nine wooden planks, enough to stand on.
My freedom as a 'free lance'.

An interstitial age. Hardly neighbourly,
I know fewer names than the years
I've been here. Rows of identikit SUVs
line the road in lieu of trees
I've seen cut back, then down.

Somewhere between coma and contentment:
well-tended green spaces; a family butcher
embarrassed by its raft of sausage circuit garlands;
too many rugby shirts around to feel at ease –
spring-evening joggers stir from hibernation.

I was the future, for a week, a while ago.
At a summer garden party, I met
a looted favourite poet:
over his empty, one-use flute, he wrangled
about the etiquette of 'watering the foliage'.

A marginal constituent, I'm more witness
than antagonist to flourishing damp.
The months pile up since my last confession;
wheels spinning slowly, hazards on,
just low enough for running down the battery.

Ethiopia Shall Stretch Forth Her Hands

Joe Louis, mid-clinch,
is lifting his opponent –
the six-foot-six 'Ambling Alp', Primo Carnera –
into the air.
In the Hague,
Italian and Ethiopian officials
have come to the end of their first day
of arbitration talks.
Here, in the Yankee Stadium,
Carnera will sink to his knees
'slowly, like a great chimney that had been dynamited'.

For breakfast this morning, Carnera consumed
a quart of orange juice, two quarts of milk,
nineteen pieces of toast, fourteen eggs,
a loaf of bread and half a pound of Virginia ham.
If he took the *Washington Post*
he would have seen a cartoon showing himself and Louis
    in the ring.
The illustrated Louis cast a dreadlocked shadow,
his shadow wore a crown.

Louis starts throwing bombs in the sixth round
and knocks the Italian down twice
before a right-left combination
ends the fight.
Louis will touch a glove to Carnera's lower back
after the bell, and return to his corner
without celebration.

Louis has been given seven commandments
by his new manager to ensure he progresses
towards a title shot unhampered
by comparisons to Jack Johnson.
He is never to have his picture taken with a white woman.
He is never to go to a nightclub alone.
There will be no soft fights.
There will be no fixed fights.
He will never gloat over a fallen opponent.
He will keep a 'dead pan' in front of the cameras.
He will live and fight clean.

In 1964, Martin Luther King Jr will write,
'More than twenty-five years ago, one of the southern
     states
adopted a new method of capital punishment.
Poison gas supplanted the gallows.
In its earliest stages, a microphone was placed inside
the sealed death chamber so that scientific observers
might hear the words of the dying prisoner.
The first victim was a young Negro.
As the pellet dropped into the container,
and the gas curled upward,
through the microphone came these words:
"Save me, Joe Louis. Save me, Joe Louis. Save me,
     Joe Louis . . ."'

The Range

'God save all here.' That's what you scored
into the metal of your childhood range.
The house was ruined when I saw it, a bored
boy of six or seven, nagging for a change
of scene as soon as we got there. Twenty
years are gone; I've not been back
to the village, the house, not for lack
of chances. Life is away, plenty
of it. You only asked that He save you. All.
You are dead, as is your mother.
Bad luck has clung to your brother
like an impermeable caul
he couldn't shake by getting out,
or having sons. He has one less. Since you.
For all the decay there was still the view
out back. Mountain family. Wiped out.

II

The blackbird is not a bad-luck bird.
The Blackbird of Avondale was not resigned
to arrears, in Kilmainham. He heard
a fresh start in letters Kitty signed
with kisses. He could not prevent Fiendish Park.
Later he could not prevent scandalising
a 'nonconformist conscience'; his larks
at Eltham almost vandalised
Home Rule. He had to go. 'If I go, I go forever.'
The 'hillside men' stayed loyal but the Master

couldn't have a mistress. Quicklime in his eyes, alive,
he sailed home for Hove and died. He was forty-five.

III

You were betrayed; there is no other way
of saying this. The doctor told you to wash your hair
and go for walks; your appetite may
or may not return. He was only too aware
of your 'nerves' and said so.
He'd delivered all seven of your daughters
after all. They told you to go
back, anti-fatted calf, for more slaughtering
neglect. He rolled your dice for you for a season.
By the time he deigned to look for the real reason
behind your winnowing it was everywhere.
The doctor told you that you'd lose your hair.

IV

There is sadness in this blackbird's song,
and I know well what tuned it wrong.
It was those by whom the deed was done.
Now all its nestlings are gone.
This type of weather I also know,
and such a loss, not long ago.
I know it well, bird, I read your state
at the sight of a home left desolate.
It was sudden they came, the callous boys,
and quick the deed your young destroys.
You and I share a fate we both deplore.
My children, like your children, are no more.

When she turned thirteen your youngest child
was plagued by neighbours seeking cures.
The seventh girl of seven girls, a wild
sort of medic, they believed, the surest
route to remedy. You did not last
to see her giving birth. A boy,
out of a house of women. The past
will find him, eventually: its joys
and scandals. He will learn about you
from her; you will be photographs
and stories. She may spare him the true
ending and choose parts to make him laugh,
like your fierce temper, the black curtain
you pinned up to con the girls to bed
with the sun still high. Or, instead,
she'll draw your life with a certain
pathos. You at seventeen, lovesick,
walking out 'to see Hughie Langan's duck',
when Hughie wasn't in, or sneaking Mick,
your stepdad, cigarettes 'for the road, and one for luck'.

VI

I found this in a book in a city you never visited:

A Charm Against Sorrow

This is a charm said by Mary for her son,
before the fair man and the turbulent woman
had laid him in the grave.
A charm that God set for himself, when the divinity
within him was darkened.
A charm to be said by the cross, when the night is black

and the soul is heavy with sorrow.
A charm to be said at sunrise, the hands on the breast,
when the eyes are red with weeping
and the madness of grief is strong.
A charm that has no words, only the silent prayer.

My mother called to say you'd gone.
I answered. She couldn't speak;
only made animal noise, a weak
throat sound which meant 'it's done'.

VII

In your dying days your daughters were visited by birds.
They stood in gardens, or entered their homes.
There were robins, for death, and blackbirds.
They are for resignation. You died at home,
light as a bird, bald as a young, blind bird.
Your children had all left but came back
to stay the night. Like your childhood
house on the hill, that home stands idle, its black
range unused also. Since you died there has been good
and bad news. More bad, I think, than good. A lot
of other leaving; the whole country is leaving, I'm told.
I could not live where the young leave before the old.
'God save all here', you wrote. You didn't say from what.

Fathers and Sons

Some thousand
Sixteen-hour workdays before you're sublime.
  – LAWRENCE JOSEPH, 'In a Fit of My Own Vividness'

All my evenings stationed
at the front door's
not-quite frosted glass:
hair flat against his head
from the hard-hat or the rain,
a watery blue shirt
torn at the armpit,
undone more than half-way down,
the patched-up vest
hanging on for another month.
My tone brighter
the further past 5 p.m.,
an assumption of traffic
or the foreman showing up
as he cleared off,
and sometimes cold lemonade,
backing away to let him drop
his lunch bag
and lever off his boots.
The transit van conspicuously bulky,
an anchor-like compressor
tethered to the streetlight;
his dinner seething
in the cooker,
first compost then char.
My mock-lightness
and half-committal punchlines,
his cooling plate of swede and cabbage

undermined by ketchup,
of bacon white-ridged
and unsalvageable,
the flourish of fruit and red jelly.
Hair washed in the kitchen sink,
the kettle whistling
about the nightly shave,
and dozing in front
of the television by 7.30 p.m.
The absence of anything like pleasure.
Finally, upstairs to put me to bed,
leading us in the song
he made up when he missed me,
about my coming back.

The Donkey

My mother kept that story near her
to belittle my father's village;
told us often how the one donkey
they'd brought into the place
hanged itself in the barn, days after market.
He bore it. Only one day she told it,
he came to my room before bed,
explained the root of it,
how when he was my age
but hardier,
not doughy with leisure but thin as rushes,
they'd bought that necessary beast
and it failed;
somehow tangled its neck in its tether.
He found it still and big-eyed
like it had seen a creature-god crouching over
with kindness in the hollow of their palm.
He still pitied it,
acting out the ass of its name in the night,
though he knew it could never have been any good,
but might through wise rutting have sired an animal
who'd take the toughness out of the day,
carry in its bones all the dormant glory
of that cheap, doomed Abraham
remembered only in spiteful jokes
and the absolute emptiness of a hayshed.

Mayfly

On the way back to the city after the long weekend,
  we stop off by prior agreement at the Mayfly,
    arrange ourselves like collapsing parachutists.
Last of the nectar days, hind-end of the country,
  the afternoon readying itself to make excuses
    and leave us to our unslept dishevelment.
Some nameless river goes by; the sun makes brilliant hoops
  from tarnished glasses. Half-picked bones;
    soporific bluebottles. To have to leave this
for the road's demands, the mercy of one last round
  not enough to delay us where people live their whole lives,
    most likely,
watch this cherry tree convulse into winter, what,
  seventy times maybe.

The Resurrection of Diego 'Chico' Corrales

Diego Corrales has risen from the canvas
and his cornerman has placed a clean gumshield in his mouth
to replace the one he spat out.

He's just been knocked down for a second time,
in this tenth round, by José Luis Castillo,
but now he's standing, and the fight resuming.
He's starting to open up
and throw heavy shots: a right cross moves Castillo,
who smiles, which means he's hurt.
Castillo is punching too, but Corrales walks through fire.

On Corrales's back is a tattoo of Christ the Redeemer.
Its arms rise and fall as he tenses his back to measure,
then land, blows on Castillo, who is sinking into the ropes,
hands lowered, no longer able to protect himself.
His head is kept up by the force of his opponent's gloves
and not the actions of his neck
when the referee steps between the men
to save him.
Corrales, having let his hands go, will not stop until he is
      stopped.

Two years from tonight, Corrales will lie dead
on the Fort Apache Road in Las Vegas,
his Suzuki motorcycle in component parts,
his license expired, his blood three times the legal alcohol
      limit.
'Bottom line, no one else did anything wrong,'
Sergeant Tracy McDonald will say,

following a report. 'He basically killed himself.'
Corrales's attorney will refer to previous drink-driving
   charges,
adding, 'It would be a shame if his memory was tarnished
at this point by past incidents.'
Castillo will say,
'Our names will be linked forever.'

Two years from tonight, but not now. Now Corrales is
   stumbling
towards a neutral corner of the ring
in the Mandalay Bay Casino.
He's being borne aloft by his trainer and his cutman,
his arms stretched out crosswise,
celebrating coming back from the dead.

Five Leaves Left

Drugs began in Aix. Those left who knew him
still talk about his hands. The size of them. His stoop

in Cambridge in a too-small new-build room;
his skin, so white you could see through it, into virginity.

They say how he was a machine, of sorts,
that the only way to get the Nick Drake guitar sound

on record would be to have Nick Drake on guitar.
He could keep it going for hours: those hands again, their
    power,

their command the last of its kind, the dead grip of Empire.
Later on, he wouldn't cut his nails, wash his clothes –

but that was down the road, that brand of sadness a hint
in the air, like the fate of apples coming into season

that will perish uneaten in their bowl. His voice
the note of goodness in the fruit, of England

lurching into colour, the trees of the forest bending their heads
like angels out of Blake, harvest time moving towards him

where he stood apart, from the detritus of a life.
He didn't like it at home but couldn't bear it anywhere else.

He was tired. He hung a future on the stopped cogs
of his alarm clock, then slept through it.

Bachelors

For cannot any man, young or old, rich or poor,
turn a few corners and bump into marriage?
– ELIZABETH HARDWICK, *Sleepless Nights*

Their wives have 'gone out shopping', and will be back
any time now, these men whose only recreation is the radio –
a little news, enough to know who's having a good season,
the budget, the weather. There was no problem with work,

when they worked, it didn't matter; digging footings,
a machine licence, sandwiches in the van at teatime. Still a few
pints of porter in the evening, among strangers, mostly,
cabbage and bacon for free on saints' days. The paper for the
    racing

but rarely a punt, the Gold Cup – sure, why not – and watch
    it in
the shop. There's always a nephew somewhere who'll visit
every few weekends with photos of his kids, leave some
    gadget
or other to gather dust. And dinner at his for Christmas

now flying's out of the question; the complications, difficult
    circulation,
the old house long closed up, now, anyway. Mice multiplying
in rooms where mothers cried them off, and were laid out,
soon enough; legal questions over deeds never resolved,
    probably

the forestry's. They break their hearts crying once or twice
at an unlikely funeral, these men, then head home for the long
evening, the one-off whiskey before bed becoming habitual.
All that sperm, useless as the priest's, who eventually visits.

From Alun Lewis

There is nothing that can save today, darling,
you not being here. You MUST write.
It's impossible to breathe otherwise.
I'm only talking of the things I really NEED.
I'm so tired of travelling away from you.
I think of you all the bloody time. Do you mind?

This isn't an answer or a letter –
it's only a cup of coffee after lunch.
Many things I've been unable to remember
came to me last night.
You sitting like a babu at a desk
in the bowels of the G.P.O.
You standing in the quartier Latin corridor
of the Hotel Marina on Sunday afternoon
after the cinema saying 'Alright, pay the taxi. Let's stay.'

When I saw you on Saturday, July 24th,
you were the flash of a sword.
Now I'm hopelessly shut into the camp life again.
A soccer match, a disjointed conversation at dinner,
a visit to the reading room to see how things go:
oh, and a longing beyond words.

There's a fat dove strutting across the lawn
by the bougainvillea.
I wish I could be strolling with you
looking at the rose moles all in stipple
upon trout that swim in your little stream.
One way or another I make a lot of shadows where I go.

Don't worry over the hairs on my head.
May you not be tried harder than you can bear.
Let there be an again, New Year.

I'm Working So I Won't Have to Try So Hard

One of those regular Friday nights upstairs at The Castle;
some of us smoking, a mixed group, most mid-twenties,
'the socialists', mainly players, a few watchers.
Emma had child-sized hands and was something in between,
measuring a few shots, losing interest. I couldn't play
to save my life, but did, cracking the cue ball
off a few pockets; the odd happy collision.
If it was Matt I didn't take my jacket off; he'd clean up
in a single visit, 'misspent youth'. Suits, no ties,
first proper job, he'd say 'unlucky, son',
he always called me 'son', and laugh like he knew
that he'd survive, years later, when he got sick.
I was better after a few bottles, most of the time,
or maybe they got worse, or went gentle.
Anyway, the window. The night I'm talking about,
I'm not sure who was first to notice; some flat
across the way, one you wouldn't have known
in daylight, it must have been late by then,
we were playing in a sort of semi-darkness,
then we were watching this couple, too far
away to make out faces, to make out ages,
but they were dancing in a bare room, kissing,
moving slow like they were three parts silk
so we could tell what was about to happen
and we envied it; we stood and watched them
kiss and dance, for a long time,
and when she turned off the light we carried on
staring at their black room, our faces looking back
from the windows of the pool bar, waiting for a sign
to carry on our games, but no sign ever came,
and there were rooms like that for all of us.

Blind Cassius and the Bear

Clay's been saying 'cut the gloves'
but Angelo Dundee continues to kneel,
to wash his face with a sponge.
Clay was blinking in round four,
and is complaining of a burning sensation.
He finished the round with his eyes shut.

He's been calling Liston a 'big, ugly bear' for months.
He's said, 'I'm ready to go to war.'
He's worked himself into a frenzy.
At the weigh-in, Clay's pulse
was 120 beats per minute.
The doctor said, 'he's scared to death.'

Clay's been linked to militant 'Black Muslims'
in the press before the fight,
costing the promoter $300,000.
One commentator's written 'Liston used to be a hoodlum;
now he is our cop.'

Clay danced, and was impossible to find
before astringent stung his eyes
but it's Liston who'll refuse to start round seven,
conceding his title on the stool.
Liston who can't raise his arms.

Clay's being pushed from his seat
by Dundee, sent out to stand in front of Liston,
blind, but by the end of the fight he'll say,
'Almighty God was with me.

I want everyone to bear witness;
I'm the greatest thing that ever lived.
I don't have a mark on my face, and I upset Sonny Liston,
and I just turned twenty-two years old.
I must be the greatest. I showed the world.
I talk to God everyday. I know the real God.
I shook up the world, I'm the king of the world.
You must listen to me.'

Tomorrow, Clay will be Cassius X
and 'Champ'.
The *New York Times* will concede that
'All those interminable refrains
of "float like a butterfly, sting like a bee"
had been more than foolish songs.'

Crisis Actor

And like you I felt sensitive and somehow apart
– ALUN LEWIS, 'To Edward Thomas'

The sullen years feeling righteously combative,
a stirred-up need for mission, a rage against the pros,
taking each line personally; Amwell Street nights
overrunning by more than their intended duration,
the Old Street speakeasy, its lukewarm cans,
hole-in-the-wall and incense burners, a loaded jazz singer
collapsing as she sang, its fire-hazard metal stairs;
the self-produced, self-published oxblood books;
the 'semi-literate phase', the beer before the launch
to this already being the best of it, but still unsatisfied;
the wanting people who wouldn't give my parents
the time of day to owe me favours.

*That whole generation who fought couldn't, or wouldn't, talk
about it. It was unbearable, unsayable, you couldn't allow
yourself to accept it, to let it become part of your life after-
wards. That was the only way to cope. These were things that
would kill you, that would make life ridiculous or impossible.
The things these men had seen had to be blanked out to allow
them to go back to their lives, to allow life to be possible.
So all that made a great impression, that inability to talk or
remember, that suppression.*

Always being drawn to Bloomsbury, to Fitzrovia,
throwing over dead-end jobs for further study,
an excuse to walk down Charlotte Street or Goodge Street,
some playacting impulse hovering among the bargain bins,
magnetised by a ghost of what had only been a ghost,
the 'Scamp' notions, the heathen pilgrimages to haunts
wipe-clean, no-tar: you wouldn't have known
the place. An urge to be part of something to the side
of what was left; a margins fetish, a letting things go by
on purpose, then by mistake; the years of afternoons,
coffees into brandies, somehow always walking in the rain
to Warren Street or Tottenham Court Road, regretting
    each step
away from whichever 'you', repression as a passion.

*He was very Bogart, consciously so. That was what he felt you
had to do – you were laconic, you didn't give anything away,
you kept your powder dry, you bought your own drinks. You
were able to cope with crises – not his own so much, but he
was very good at being strong on other people's behalf. You
have a duty to one another. It can't be overestimated, the im-
pact that had, what he thought masculinity was, what it meant
to be a man. The reality of it was that men couldn't talk about
what they'd seen, and there was a sense that there wasn't much
to say now.*

Thinking back to another, remembered summer,
its sudden 'she', lunchtimes lying in Russell Square,
our enthused contortions,
life for a while gentle, almost pastoral,
or outside the Tavern, strong gins
and her in sunglasses with her arms out,
basking like a tomcat in the warm patch,
cigarette smoke dropping like crematorium ash.
A brief sense of coming home; of fellow feeling,
familiar zealotry and recklessness,
the not-quite-above-board, corner-of-the-Square
kisses. The feeling of a train run off its rails
and waking in the sidings; a night of taking away
sharp objects, things being no longer ideal;
the heart not in it again after, the turning off,
preferring not to, the not-so-great refusals.

*I have this memory, still quite vivid, of coming upon him –
it was a beautiful summer weekend – lying on his back in a
cornfield looking up at the sky and it seemed to me this was
the maybe too cornily obvious embodiment of the romantic
poet side, that this was what he felt. Maybe he just wished
he could be that rather than what he actually felt he was, but
there it was – that wasn't the winged avenger, that was the very
exposed, vulnerable, open to anything that might come and
screw you up side of things. A lot of my memories of those
early days are of him in that aspect, rather than of the tougher
side of things.*

An autumn afternoon spent in the house,
going through last notebooks, crabbed handwriting:
'Later work'; 'heartaches or just chest pains';
'in general terms I'm looking out for her, as usual'.
Your Arnold streak, your feeling of disaster in the air,
your trouble with money, low centre of gravity,
quiet voice and coat left on indoors,
your feeling you existed only if called upon to serve,
your somehow getting to be forty, the crappy things
you'd have to do if you didn't do that crappy thing;
'Projected books, half-thoughts, the children's birthdays',
then something urgent, all else dissolved away.

*He had his feet utterly on the ground but he did have a sort
of irrational, I think in the end it's no more than a poetic or
genuinely imaginative streak that sees beyond, or believes in
seeing beyond, the daily categorising and ways we talk about
things. And this has obviously been a huge issue in modern
culture, that so much of the way we live is handed over to
instrumentality, practical things, doing things and so on and
there's so little that's intuitive, you could call it magical, I sup-
pose, mysterious.*

'It's all about goodbyes, or being late . . .
I know that you won't let me call it love.'

Bar Italia

I know the place. Rarely in the day,
usually down the back, among *tifosi* – inhumanists:
their one true love the shirt, its primary colours.
I've been here with different yous, nothing lasted –
beer at silver tables, the bells of midnight warming
up their throats, leopard jackets,
summer air a song about late light, God in violet
heaven; *amaretto, amaretti, amaratt* . . .
This morning at the bar, Rocky Marciano
makes eye contact from the cave of his record.
Monochrome, hermetic, perfected – he knows
what this over-priced coffee means to say:
start over, *cuore rosso*, today is young,
anywhere but here it might seem possible, etc.

My Son, the Heart of My Life

Joe Louis came to Brockton once
to referee an amateur bout.
Rocco Marchegiano – a local boy
who didn't want to grow up to smell of leather
like his father –
followed Louis to the restroom with a friend.
Rocco was boosted up to get a better look,
earning half a dollar when he was spotted.

Rocky Marciano has almost every strike
against him.
Two left feet.
Stoop-shouldered.
A 68-inch reach.
Not starting out until he was ancient,
nearly twenty-five, Rocky was so raw his trainer tied string
to his feet to help him keep his balance.

Rocky trains in an aeroplane hangar,
staying there for two months before a fight.
He denies his body all the things he loves
and hits a custom-made 300-pound bag
which makes any man he'll meet seem portable.
He jogs ten miles of hill a day,
sprinting up and back, dipping low to generate power.
He swims shoulder-deep, punching water.
A week before a fight Rocky takes no calls,
eats no new food, reads no mail,
shakes no hands.

At the height of his championship reign
the US testing company will be contracted
to measure the power in his hands.
They'll have him throw a right into a machine;
the energy behind his punch
will be equivalent to an armour-piercing shell.

It has just retired Joe Louis,
knocking him through the ropes
in Madison Square Garden.
Louis is a helpless figure, head tilted back,
eyes turned towards the ceiling lights.
Sugar Ray Robinson is running down the aisle to hug him,
and see if he's all right.

Rocky will retire undefeated,
saying, 'I didn't never really get hurt in the ring,
and I feel perfect physically
and probably still had two or three good fights left.'

On the night before his forty-sixth birthday
when a private plane he is travelling in
hits a tree near Newton, Iowa,
Rocky will be decapitated.
An investigation into the circumstances
will conclude that 'the pilot attempted an operation
exceeding his experience and ability'.

When Marciano's mother is told the news she will say
'*Figlio mio, figlio mio, core di mamma!*'
Joe Louis will kiss the lid of the closed casket,
look at the ceiling of the funeral home,
and say, 'Something's gone out of my life. I'm not alone;
something's gone out of everyone's life.'

Someone will run down the aisle to hug him,
and see if he's all right.

Colin Falck

I met you late in the day,
already decades deep into reasoning the unknown into
    the known
of which we are possessed (that royal 'we').
Garden Suburb Zen master, one outfit did the job,
trainers snazzier than ascetic utility,
silver ankh at once charm and pendulum.
So much for located experience,
three moves in a decade –
each house plush, dark, book-lined
(the key texts could have lived with just two shelves):
'We won't find the poems of Robert Frost
in *The Poetry of Robert Frost.*'
I only saw the front rooms,
attending, monthly, for unadjusted impressions,
hopeful your side lamp would at least stay on
beyond the throat-clearing cough,
the common-sense dismissal,
the exiling of tangents to various, permanently deferred,
'sub-committees'.
An odd combination of manic hyperactivity
and morbid decline – your verdict on modern poetry
and, in the end, your fate; rude health
until it wasn't, one morning on Leigh Hunt's Heath.
Evenings begun with piano recitals from a surprising
toddler – your own late harvest –
expensive cats, like their owner,
hardly domestic, rare, unimpressable.

You were dear to me,
devoted to art beyond nicety,
head full of singing lines learned with use, not design.
We who sat at your table were lucky,
taking our anonymous, instantly recognisable, turns
out of the ancient envelope.
Not enough years for your plans,
Coleridgean fancy, Arnoldian faith,
philosophy background of 'a slightly unorthodox kind',
the camper van idling outside,
in anticipation of some grander removal.
'Are there any other angles on this?'

The Young God of the Catskills 1

Mike Tyson is twenty years, four months and twenty-two
    days old
and in the dressing room of the Hilton Hotel.
He's breaking down his gloves:
pushing the leather to the back,
so his knuckles can pierce through.
He's afraid of everything.
During training he's been afraid of the world champion,
Trevor Berbick.
He's dreamed of Berbick beating him.
'The closer I get to the ring
the more confident I get,' he will later explain.
'Once I'm in the ring I'm a god.'

'I try to catch them right on the tip of the nose,
because I try to punch the bone into the brain.
People don't have the slightest idea
of just how hard it is
to break somebody's jaw or eye socket.
They think it's just the power.
But it's the accuracy of the power.
Every punch is thrown with bad intention and the speed of
    the devil.'

It will take Tyson five minutes and thirty-five seconds
to dispose of Berbick.
The final punch,
a left to Berbick's temple,
will knock the champion down three times:
Berbick's brain won't accept he's finished.

The first time he'll fall flat on his back
in the centre of the ring.
The second, he'll collapse sideways into the ropes.
The third time he will fall
forwards, failing to extend his hands
in time to save his face.

Tyson will celebrate with a shrug,
a kiss on the lips of his manager.
'My record will last for immortality.
It will never be broken.
It's ludicrous these mortals even attempt to enter my realm.'

Years on, believing God to be a regular visitor
to his apartment and himself the world champion,
Berbick will be attacked
by a twenty-year-old with a length of pipe
and left to die in a churchyard.
Fifty-two at the time of his death, according to boxing
     records;
some reports will have him as fifty-six, others as forty-nine.
'Legally, I'm a spirit,' he will say between this night
and that. 'I have no age.'

Seated Nude Girl with Pigtails (1910)

Most meetings are coincidence or instantly forgotten;
analysis starts with the result, then rewrites the game.
I would like to be alone with someone in the evening;
a few drinks, a smoke, a companionable dawn chorus.
No fatalist – a life is going on somewhere which I'll encroach
    upon
in time. I may know it already, in other contexts.
I have my suspicions. Like when you leaned
back in your seat, framing your face with an arm.
Not desire, not yet, just close attention:
seeing that your hands move like naked, articulate creatures;
noticing how you gather your hair; I think about some
    evening
down the line, coming home to you. What that might be like.
All the while waiting for the lightning strike which won't be
    seen
till post-production, like a god, or any ordinary monster.

Pretty Boy Blues

You won't remember this – one evening, typically throwaway,
you said I couldn't, strictly speaking, be a failed writer,
never having written. This would have been Rory's, after
   practice,
that estate with some pastoral name –
a dog, or wolf, we never saw it, barking threats
below the window. It'd be easy to say that was your
philosophy training talking – that being another shower
you passed through, and came out dry.

The first time we met we launched straight in:
an unlocked squash court at the Union,
you working out all the chords in seconds.
Those afternoons, those evenings, boil down to flashes.
Did we rehearse? I know we played that Friday
at The Slavonics, where you convinced the crowd and me
you were something to Lomax, your – allegedly, believably
his – 'Pretty Boy Blues' going down a storm. Your green hat.

Our performances are all overlaid now.
You picking out 'Saturday Sun' on Nick Drake's anniversary,
having something of him about you, his fine bones.
Am I making up long hair? The accorgion feels later,
after the 'classic line-up'. The Watershed
has stayed more or less whole – our finest hour, I'd say. Did
say, often. I seemed to spend a lot of time trying
to convince you we should do more. Your insightful
   demurrals.

You were fully formed, though I couldn't
place it, then. A taste for Thomas Mann, solo walking
    holidays,
pedantry and contrarianism.
I suppose the loss of guitar and piano hurt less, having been
    so lightly
carried, though nothing you did made you break sweat,
not even 'trying to fancy' someone. At least you got songs
    out of that.
And you picked pity as the worst human quality;
you wanted it outlawed, holding yourself to higher standards.

Sometimes you aren't in the picture
but you must have been. The evening
it snowed while we recorded, we came out into a city
shocked white, then walked to The Lamb, but I couldn't
    face it.
I was sulkingly bovine; you were knowing about spices
and Mexico, coming back from a week in Sennybridge
with some of the best songs I'd ever heard,
dropping them as easily as sending us a postcard.

All that time spent trying to impress you, not noticing
you didn't do impressed, some quieter sort of approval,
implicit in your being in the room. Only one time
you seemed vulnerable, when you'd turned your head
for a colleague, the teaching years, were trying to decide
whether to love her and then voting against it. You asked
    to play
a song for her at one of my nights, at Filthy's, one of the first
    haunts.
The last time I heard you, maybe the last time anyone did.

By the time Rory and I came to see you in Keele – still largely
unexplained – it was steroid injections for your joints,
a digital camera and – distrusted – counselling course,
your new, barely extending, extensions. Off the pills
for the weekend so you could drink (not much, never much),
you took our hands as we walked the greenest section,
swinging in between us, our beautiful boy, unembarrassable,
instinctive leadership intact among the yellowhammers.

The Young God of the Catskills 11

It's just after 9 a.m. local time in Tokyo.
Tyson's cornerman has filled a condom with ice water
and is pressing it against his fighter's eye.
There's no enswell
because no one thought to bring one.

James 'Buster' Douglas, a 42/1 outsider,
isn't scared of the champion.
His mother died twenty-three days ago
but he refused to cancel his title shot.
Tyson's barely trained.
'You thought I was Caesar,
you thought I was Caligula out there in Japan.'

Because of the time,
and the Japanese fans' politeness,
the arena has been in near silence through the opening
    rounds.
It will stay quiet when Tyson drops Douglas in the eighth
and when he struggles to his feet.
When Douglas pivots in the tenth to land the blow
which knocks Tyson down for the first time in his career,
the stadium will remain 'so quiet
you could have heard a rat pissing on cotton'.

Years from now, Douglas will say,
'My main strategy was to survive.
My corner said he was going to come like hell
and I was ready for that challenge.
I thought Tyson was getting up

until I had seen him looking for that mouthpiece
and then I knew he was really hurt.'

Tyson will say,
'I just stopped caring.
He got up. Nobody else had.'

The Rat

Only the rat: that's all I can remember,
from the whole of the day we spent together.
Not the gallery, not stopping off for coffee,
just walking along the river, the rocky strip,
and coming upon the rat.

That's all, is it?

Yes, at this distance from it, that's the only
thing left of the day. It was white
and bloated with water, flat out on a stone
in supplication. I would have stepped on it
if not for a shout from my friend.

That's something at least, not stepping on it.

It is. That's one good thing. I looked down
for a second or two when she screamed
and saw its head thrown back, its teeth
over its jaw. I'm nearly sure I saw veins
under the fur but that may be invention.

That can happen, you can misremember a thing.

You can, an unpleasant thing especially,
it can sour further when it's thought about.
I remember my friend's face, how she was frozen,
pointing but unable to say a word. She saw it
first, the rat. I had been talking to her.

At least she saw it, and stopped you doing worse.

She did and it's lucky that she picked it out;
it was daylight and not easy to spot
against the grey. Already I see how it'll go;
I'm worried the whole summer will eventually
be remembered for that rat. The whole year, even.

It'll be a while before the whole year, surely?

It might, but it could happen. The memory
isn't easy to control. Where I'd want to think
of happier things I've no choice in the matter,
which is why I'm so concerned. A sight like that
can wipe out a thousand smaller, better ones.

You didn't stand on it, at least, that's something.

It is, you're right. I must focus now on that.

Keats Parade

A little 'Endymion' projected under the railway bridge for a
  few months
against posters of phone tariffs, IKEA's annunciation and a
  small parade:
it only worked in winter, dark by commuting-time, the hi-vis
jackets of travel-sized community supporters out in all their
  (limited) force,

the newly built bus garage a staging post or track meet for
  grudge matches,
mostly settled by evening, in time for the council tax-payers
to make landfall: a residual rusty bloodstain or two, the
  perennial floral tributes
and cardboard signs, felt-tip and text-speak, more fallen
  soldiers to be put away,

a dawning awareness of two sets of occupants on the same
  tracks – like toys
come alive at night, or an oversold aeroplane – it could all
  pass me by,
unless I watched the news, or stayed out past six. The petrol
  station
where rematches broke out; the shop that changed business
  model

on a bi-monthly basis, settling for a while on a range of
  leisurewear,
curtains, bleach and the same five lettuces; a 'hair saloon'
  staffed by bodybuilders

who took turns to smoke and intimidate drivers; the bicycle-
 repair shop
open twenty-four hours, all its stock heaped outside to make
 room for the crowds;

the flagrant daylight hand-to-hand exchanges; the ever-bulkier
 status dogs
of the suit-jacket and tracksuit types who ran a snooker club
 with barred door
and swollen membership, then put them to pasture in a yard
 backing onto my street,
fur curly and unkempt, like a teen idol, leaking just-following-
 orders spit 'n' drool;

the constant threats of permit parking to offset fights over
 space –
the work-around first of traffic cones then wheelie bins,
 rolled out to save
a spot, the inevitable passive-aggression, then aggressive-
 aggression,
the afternoon of the samurai sword, the afternoon of the
 rumoured shooting,

the many mornings after the actual shootings and constant
 helicopters
and through-the-night sound system wakes; the finding out
 most of the worst
weeks later, when I needed a haircut, from a barber who
 made more selling
second-hand vinyl than cutting hair, his sign in eight languages
 refusing credit

or queue-jumping, his xenophobia permitting itself a
 Lithuanian girlfriend,

his shop beneath an empty dojo, shuttered after he came to
    the attention
of those from whom protection should be sought. Go-square
    for each new raft
of incomers; starting blocks we, for various reasons, never
    took off from,

having failed to hear the pistols or having run far enough,
    for long enough.
Where, when I have to, they have to take me in . . . all of
    childhood
going on amongst it and never realising what was happening
    just outside:
head-down in my unprotesting orbit, shuttling between
    school, church

and relatives; no street-life to speak of, lowered-risk, eyes
    watching God
or Italian football on Sundays; books, homework and solo
    indoor pursuits,
never – lucky, sheltered, oblivious – darkening the door of
    J. Day & Son,
traditional memorials: its granite, firemen calendar, tail-end
    of 'a joy for ever'.

Rope-a-Dope

Nothing for days, then a message:
'I want to see a fight. An old one.'
So I bring a fight to you.
You know nothing of these men;
even the most famous
get to slink in their youth again –
for you Foreman is Leviathan, unstoppable;
Ali just past his prime
flown 'home' to muscle back his title.
Not sure how you'll react to violence,
we lie down again together –
your feet in woollen stockings
kneadable across my thighs,
your mouth close to my ribs
and their inmate: a pouting lifer.
Ali opens up with right-hand leads, you flinch
but soon you're lost to the screen
where he waits it out along the ropes,
takes everything Foreman throws.
You don't believe he can soak up
all this pain and go on standing;
we cheer him on,
winter softened in the tropic of his strength.
When Ali comes alive to put Foreman on the ground
I see a Hallelujah look as you turn to face me:
'He won,' you say into my cheek.
'He did,' I say.

It's a Long Way Back from Nowhere

My one-time desk-mate – our shared berth for several months
between my several leavings, most of them in silence – lupine,
angular. Watford. Some chance reading material, Patrick
Hamilton's

Hangover Square: 'I had a single called that.' If not a floodgate
at least a trickle. The odd half in the Three Kings, discussing
his canon, by now petrified and European, almost nothing

in colour. A few rebirths already, the latest into bossa nova
with a Swede, his current Jane Birkin, begun when she asked
for a signature at a festival and it was the least he could do.

Routines, the same snack each day at the same time, the same
T-shirts on rotation, hoops mostly, the same lunchtime
roll-up on the same bench, the same rain, months

of rain despite my sticking it more than a season.
Lou Reed's *Berlin* he could bear, some of Van Dyke Parks'
orchestration. A lot of Smog. 4.30 p.m. finish each day, going
early

on flexitime, setting off for a trudge over Shoot Up Hill.
Coming in with snatches of Larkin. 'Love Again' he liked,
humour less gallows than abattoir, a staff Christmas outing

on the London Eye, Charlton's stadium lights on, on a
Thursday:
'burning foreigners'. Idea for a country album: *It's a Long Way
Back from Nowhere*. A former collaborator in a floating
prison.

Before it all went west with the Swede, I got to see him live,
a long-since-shuttered place on Kilburn High Road:
lightly androgynous and comfortable, under red-tinted lights,

his songs *l'esprit d'escalier* for guitar, the reflection of silver
off his strings when he paused made it seem like he held
starlight in his hands, and was translating it to bone.

Jehovah and the River

Patrice Lumumba, 'the greatest black man
who ever walked the African continent',
was bound in ropes,
en route to trial in Leopoldville,
to start Mobutu Sese Seko's rise to power.
The CIA wanted Lumumba's head
but could not complete the job;
it fell to the man Reagan will one day call
'a voice of good sense and goodwill'
to dull the point of a sickle-sponsored hook.
Pictures of Mobutu,
'epitome of a closet sadist',
are everywhere you look.

Under the 100,000-seater stadium
detention rooms were built.
Mobutu had a thousand criminals
rounded up to fill his pens,
then a hundred picked at random to be killed.
Career criminals forge connections
to protect them when in trouble:
Mobutu proved these connections' worth.
He was Jehovah.

When it was over, the monsoons came.
Before the fight, Ali said, 'we're going to dance'.
Instead, he lay along the ropes,
'loose as a goose' in the heat,
letting the undefeated Foreman
exhaust himself with scores of clubbing blows.

Ali taunted him throughout:
'They told me you punch as hard as Louis'
and, 'Is that all you've got?'
Later, Ali will say,
'Foreman couldn't look me in the eyes at first
and when he did, he looked deep.
Then he knew – he knew I was someone different.'

The rain in Kinshasa is so heavy
had it started at the bell
Ali and Foreman could have drowned.
The press corps riding through the night
see crowds lining the road;
crowds are leaping up and down.
News has started to go round.
What happened here is going to shock the world.

Promises Had Been Made

Sam Cooke was being murdered
in the bar of the Corinthia,
another retromaniac crooning
this year's theme-tune: *If you ever change your mind* . . .
You had your Yeats by heart.
You said you'd butcher it, and sure enough
paused, and started lines again.
I didn't have it to compare
so when you spoke in a low voice
I was convinced you were writing on air.

A few days gone we stood out on your roof,
between Big Ben and Nelson.
Promises had been made
about the moon.
It was caught behind cloud and seemed no fuller
than it ever had,
no nearer than before.
There were clouds across us two,
made of the obscuring months
we passed beneath the same constellations.

I took on faith your saying
it was the brightest it will ever be,
drawing in as close as it was able.
On faith, I would accept you as the brightest
in my span of years,
the future swinging
whatever light's still left in its bone lantern.
Apparently we're already old enough

for it to mean this won't happen again
in our lifetime.

Halcyon Days

There's only one time when you were perfect for loving in life,
and if you miss that time, if you ignore it or pass it by, you've
really missed something.

— JAMES SALTER

I

Autumn wind, the leaves a golden mash
at our feet in the kind, quiet blaze
of the streetlight; I am taking your arm
under the umbrella, leaning into you,
waiting, imagining sweet violences.
My tongue is stoppered; its unfamiliar
ecstasies. I cannot say any of this
here, in ordinary streets, in the woods
around home, walking into the warmth
and taking off my woollen hat,
putting on records.
I can only take off one glove and press
my palm to your cheek, for a moment,
a sort of sigh, the whole world made
of lavender and foxglove, of those dreams
we have but don't discuss, of bedsheets
and mornings, our circling talk.
I call you old Zeus, your big, noble head,
your serious heart I haven't yet dived
through, even after everything;
Primrose Hill, that dream of fireworks and port
and staying on the train. I want to hear you say it,
that we're the children of a king
and we've nowhere to go but a cottage built
on other people's sorrow.

And now you're leaving me to find out
what's in store? You talk of fate, of oracles:
this is the future, here. You have no need
of seers. What was that, on the Heath,
your last birthday, a willow tree for heaven,
our legs entwined, the cricket songs of June – you
smelled of soap and sun cream and we were still
nervous of each other. You think there's another
path? If you have to find it out
I'll come with you. You think I fear the sea,
that wrecking clown; I'd sooner face
the fiercest waves than see you off, handkerchief
in hand. If what waits is death, let's both
meet it: being here alone is worse than that,
the sudden silence, not knowing if you'll come.

III

I've come to know the morning, first light
in the window, fussing around, making endless
tea. You not here is impossible; I want to send
a note, a ghost message, I can't bear not speaking,
not knowing how to reach you. It's Friday
morning and it's snowing and I've just walked
through the white woods to the station
and I wish you were coming round this afternoon
to talk about the snow, and have toast,
and sit with me with the fire on, and tell me
about your worries because I do quite miss you.

IV

I've been preparing to have you back, trying on dresses,
darning the old reliables, the gloves you left; I'm fixing
up the drawers, all busy work. These past nights I haven't
seen you, and it's made me feel afraid,
but now you've come to me again.
There's something unfamiliar in your face,
this isn't how you move, as if a stranger
was impersonating, uncannily – but still, I'd know
you anywhere. Why are you so pale, dear heart,
what is it that you want to say? What's this
dullness in your eye, this slow and faltering speech?

V

So this is what we're left, these seven days a year,
the wind died down around us, enough to
live on, just about. Lighter, no less in love,
glutted on the memory of being young,
our onetime flesh. You made a promise early on,
to pretend I wasn't all your daylight,
that the world's voice was no louder than the peace
we'd briefly found, that you didn't know I'd walk out
on it all, and wanted to. That I chose you.

VI

I've come down to the shore,
the pebbled place I saw you last, the last spot
where you held me; it was here, I think,
these very stones, your shadow fell across that final
time, where mine now falls, alone, stretching
its arms towards you, further than I can.
How can you be gone when I still love you?
When I can call out to you in whichever tense
I choose. Come home.

VII

Though it's so far off I know it's you,
that you've returned. Before I pause to think
I'm wading out, the sea is ice,
I'm packed for the grave
as yesterday's catch. Kingfisher,
heart's bird, I dive into your death
like catching headfirst fish. I swallow
all your scales and feel alive.

Thunder

'Irish' Micky Ward has made the five-hour trip
from Lowell, MA, to Canastota, NY,
to induct Arturo 'Thunder' Gatti into the Hall of Fame.
It's ten years since their last fight:
that night when Gatti broke his hand on Ward's hip
but carried on. Round ten began with an embrace,
before the last of thirty rounds spent trying
to put each other on a gurney.
For the final minute, the commentator
said little more than 'they rise again in Boardwalk Hall'.

Gatti always said his toughest test would come
when he met someone like himself,
but outside the ring, and later in the night,
Gatti was the wilder one.
He lived in go-go bars; breakfast was three Percocets;
his drinking dented $16 million purses;
loaded up a shotgun wedding overlooking the Grand Canyon
with a dancer half his age who called him *mi amor*.
When Gatti's body was discovered
at a resort in Pernambuco
his love was held for murder.

Despite a history of 'domestic unrest'
and alleged 'suicidal tendencies',
Ward couldn't believe Gatti knew how to quit.
Walking past the coffin, Ward touched it with a hook:
'I got you last'.

'I think about him every day at some point,' Ward says,
in Canastota. 'It's like when stars align,
that was me and him. For what reason I don't know.
Arturo will be a part of me forever.
The memories will be in my mind forever.
Our fights will stay in my head forever.
So we'll be together forever.'

Jonathan Rendall

I prefer losers. They're more self-aware.
— Twelve Grand

He boxed well enough to write about it, hated winning
enough to be a gambler. Small wins were the worst;
ride the blue curve or lump it all on, lose, feel elated:
twelve bags on the nags, slots, coin toss;
boom-time Cuba Libres in Cuba, full immersion;
always a change into old costumes, 'the real test
of life, actually', to come back in new conditions.

Relationships real, invented, elaborated, ended with notes:
'I AM A STRAY DOG, BUT YOU WOULDN'T CHUCK
A STRAY DOG OUT THE WAY YOU DO ME. SIGNED:
    STRAY DOG.'
Lifelong silent war against pragmatists, diminished patience
for the hurt business, its superstructure, its easy flow,
'like riding on a sewer in a glass-bottomed boat'.
'Poetry won, and it always would', except his own,

to a 28/1 outsider, fifth at the Derby until its exhausted
chestnut cartwheel, tent, injection. Near enough to
    Newmarket
to test the going with bricks dropped in the garden;
the long-mooted biography of Tyson,
a man with 'the tendency to take on aspects of other people's
    identities',
commission, stall, can, repeat; a laying down of arms,
somewhere in the neighbourhood of January.

Trinity Hospital

There was a gunboat on the river
when you led me to your new favourite spot:
a home for retired sailors;
squat, white, stuccoed,
with a golden bell.

It could have been a lost Greek chapel,
a monument to light,
designed to remind the old boys
of their leave on Aegean shores
among tobacco and fruit trees.

Just after rain,
sunlight stood between us
like a whitewashed wall.
You were lit skin, gilt
and honey, dressed in olive.

No paper trail connects us.
No procedure of law
would tell you where to stand
in your sleek black mourning dress
if I were to die

but as you turned towards me
the golden bell rang to witness
that I, being of sound mind,
will be delivered through orange groves
to you, the white church of my days.

Notes

A number of the boxing poems contain found material from contemporary and historical newspaper reports, boxing magazines, interviews, documentaries and other related sources. The Martin Luther King Jr quotation in 'Ethiopia Shall Stretch Forth Her Hands' is from *Why We Can't Wait* (New American Library, 1964). Several of the poems were previously collected in *Fighters, Losers* (New Walk, 2019).

Part IV of 'The Range' is a version of the twelfth-century Irish poem 'Cumhthach Labhras an Lonsa' ('It Is Sadly the Blackbird Calls').

'Mayfly' is for Will Burns.

'From Alun Lewis' uses material from Alun Lewis's letters to Freda Aykroyd, collected in *A Cypress Walk* (Enitharmon, 2006).

'Crisis Actor' is *in memoriam* Ian Hamilton. The prose sections are from interviews by the author with Colin Falck and Alan Jenkins.

'Bar Italia' is for Hugo Williams.

'*Seated Nude Girl with Pigtails* (1910)' takes its title from an Egon Schiele painting and was commissioned by S. J. Fowler for his Kakania project.

Acknowledgements

Thanks are due to the editors of the following publications in which versions of some of these poems have appeared previously: *Ambit*, *The Forward Book of Poetry 2022*, *Liberties*, London Review Bookshop blog, *The New Statesman, Poetry* (Chicago), *Poetry London, The Poetry Review, Rough Trade Magazine, The Social Gathering, The Spectator, Structo, Subtropics, Test Centre, The Times Literary Supplement, The White Review* and *Wild Court*.

Especial thanks to Robert Selby, André Naffis-Sahely, Will Burns, Malene Engelund, Liz Berry and Tarn MacArthur; to Alan Jenkins for helping to shape the book into what it is; to Lavinia Singer, Matthew Hollis, Jane Feaver and Kate Burton at Faber; to Hannah Sullivan, Catharine Morris, Stephen Knight, John Clegg, Catherine Hamilton, Isabel Galleymore, Rory Waterman and Boris Dralyuk; to teachers/ mentors Andrew Motion, Jo Shapcott, Mark Ford and David Harsent; to Sarah Chalfant, Luke Ingram and Alba Ziegler-Bailey at the Wylie Agency; and to my family and friends.